Targeting Maths
Dictionary

Garda Turner

PASCAL
PRESS

Targeting Maths – Maths Dictionary
Written by Garda Turner
© Blake Publishing 2003
Reprinted 2004, 2005, 2006 (twice), 2008, 2009, 2010

ISBN 978 1 92072 814 4

Published by:
Pascal Press
PO Box 250
Glebe   NSW   2037
www.pascalpress.com.au

Publisher: Katy Pike
Series editor: Garda Turner
Editor: Amanda Santamaria

Illustrations by Luke Jurevicius
Photos by Paul McEvoy, Comstock, Corbis, Digital Vision, Eyewire, Flat Earth,
Image Library, Photodisc, Rubberball, Stockbyte, Trimensions

Designed and typeset by The Modern Art Production Group
Printed by Green Giant Press

Introduction

The *Targeting Maths Dictionary* is an essential guide to the mathematical language and concepts used in Australian primary schools. It has been written with the young reader in mind, giving clear, simple and concise definitions. Most definitions also include a colourful photo or diagram to assist understanding. Worked examples offer further explanation. The words covered come from all strands of the primary mathematics curriculum.

This book is a handy, easy-to-use and easy-to-carry reference for all young students. Many everyday words take on a special meaning when we use them in mathematics. This can be confusing for students. Understanding mathematical language and symbols is an integral part of learning many mathematical concepts. The dictionary will also aid parents when they are assisting their children at home.

Useful reference charts include mathematical symbols, abbreviations, fraction tables, metric measurement tables, conversion from metric to Imperial measure and Roman numerals.

Contents

abacus
- an instrument made of rods and beads
- used for counting

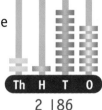

Th H T O
2 186

acre
- an Imperial measurement used for measuring the area of large blocks of land

Fields were measured in acres.

acute angle
- an angle that measures between 0° and 90°

add
- to combine things
- join together

addition
- to combine two or more numbers to make one larger number

7 + 12 + 9 = 28

adjacent
- next to each other

a b
a and b are adjacent angles.

algebra
- a part of mathematics where letters or symbols are used instead of numbers

$\blacklozenge \div 8 = 64$

$42 + y = 52$

algorithm
- the formal way of setting out operations to work out the answer

```
  2 9 4
- 1 6 7
_____
```

This is a subtraction algorithm.

am
- stands for ante meridiem
- means the time from midnight to midday (morning)

sunrise

1

A

analog clock or watch
– a clock or watch that shows twelve-hour time

angle
– the amount of turning between two straight lines (arms) that are fixed at a point

annual
– once every year

anticlockwise
– moving in the opposite direction to the hands on a clock

apex
– the vertex that is furthest from the base

approximation
– very close but not exact

> 200 is an approximation for 197.

arc
– a part of the circumference of a circle

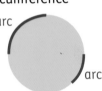

area
– the size of a surface
– the space inside a boundary

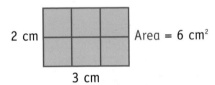

2 cm   Area = 6 cm²

3 cm

arms (of an angle)
– the two straight lines that form an angle

array
– objects or numbers arranged in rows and columns

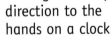

A

ascending order
– in order from smallest to largest

25, 85, 109, 153, 286

These numbers are written in ascending order.

associative law
– two or more numbers can be added (or multiplied) in any order

6 + 12 + 4 is the same as
4 + 6 + 12 or 12 + 6 + 4

2 × 9 × 5 is the same as
2 × 5 × 9 or 9 × 5 × 2

asymmetry
– has no lines of symmetry

This figure has asymmetry.

attribute
– a characteristic of an object
– can be size, colour, thickness, length etc.

a long, pink, round candy bar

autumn
– the season that follows summer
– March, April, May

average
– is one score that tries to show the 'middle' of a group of scores
– to find the average add all the scores and divide by how many scores there are

The average of 5, 9, 11, 7 and 8 is (5 + 9 + 11 + 7 + 8) ÷ 5 = 8

axis (graph)
– a scaled line that is a reference line

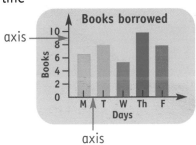

3

B

balance scales

bar graph
– a graph drawn in one bar

Pet Shop Sales

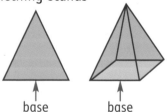

| Dogs | Cats | Birds | Fish |

base
– a line or surface on which something stands

base   base

billion
– a thousand millions

$$1\ 000 \times 1\ 000\ 000 = 1\ 000\ 000\ 000$$

bisect
– to divide something into two equal parts

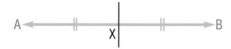

Line AB is bisected at X.

brackets
– symbols used to group things together

$$(9 + 5) \times (7 - 3) = 56$$

Brackets group 9 and 5 together, and 7 and 3 together.

breadth
– another name for width

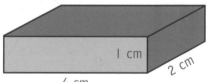

1 cm

4 cm   2 cm

The breadth is 2 cm.

calculate
– to work something out

Calculate how much money was spent to buy these items.

9c + 27c + 18c = 54c

calculator
– a machine that works out mathematical equations

calendar
– a time map that tells us what day and month it is

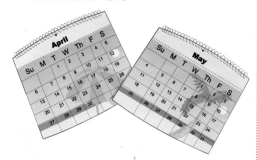

capacity
– how much something holds
– is measured in millilitres (mL), litres (L) and kilolitres (kL)

This container has a capacity of 2 litres.

Celsius
– a temperature scale that is used to tell how hot or cold something is
– water boils at 100°C and freezes at 0°C

centicube
– a block that is 1 cm wide, 1 cm long and 1 cm deep

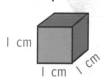

1 cm
1 cm 1 cm

centimetre
– a measurement used for measuring length
– abbreviation is **cm**

0   1   2   3   4   5

centimetres

5

c

centre
– the middle
– the midpoint of a circle

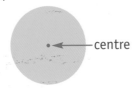

centre

century
– 100 years

We are living in the 21st century
(from 2 000 – 2 099).

chord
– a straight line in a circle that
goes from one point on the
circumference to another point on
the circumference but does not go
through the centre

chord

circle
– a 2D shape that has one curved
edge only

circumference
– the curved edge
of a circle

circumference

classify
– arrange in groups according to
attributes

These flowers are classified
according to colour.

clockwise
– moving in the
same direction
as the hands
on a clock

column
– a vertical arrangement of figures

93
42
7
19

column graph

– a graph that represents the data in a series of vertical or horizontal columns

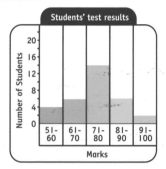

Students' test results

common denominator

– a denominator that all fractions in a group can be changed to

One common denominator for $\frac{1}{2}$, $\frac{1}{3}$, $\frac{1}{4}$ is 12.

$\frac{1}{2} = \frac{6}{12}$, $\frac{1}{3} = \frac{4}{12}$, $\frac{1}{4} = \frac{3}{12}$

commutative law

– when adding (or multiplying) numbers it does not matter in what order they are added (or multiplied)

6 + 8 is the same as 8 + 6.

17 × 23 × 6 is the same as 6 × 23 × 17.

compass

– an instrument that tells us direction

compass points

– the main points are north, south, east, west

– then north-east, south-east, south-west, north-west

– then north-north-east, east-north-east, east-south-east, south-south-east, south-south-west, west-south-west, west-north-west, north-north-west

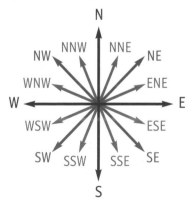

compasses (a pair of)
– an instrument used
to draw circles or arcs

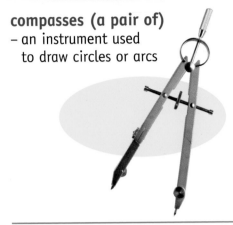

compensation strategy
– to add (or subtract) a bigger or
smaller number then adjust the
answer

$$27 + 83 = 27 + 80 + 3$$
$$87 - 39 = 87 - 40 + 1$$

complementary angles
– two angles whose sum is 90°

25° and 65° are
complementary angles.

composite number
– a number which has more than
two factors

10 has factors of 1, 2, 5 and 10.

10 is a composite number.

concentric circles
– two or more circles which have
the same centre

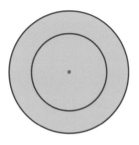

cone
– a 3D object that has a
circular base and
one vertex

congruent
– having exactly the same size and
shape

These balls are
congruent.

These triangles are
congruent.

consecutive numbers
– numbers which follow one another

17, 18, 19, 20
are consecutive numbers.

converging lines

– two or more lines that meet at one point

coordinates

– two numbers (or letters) which tell position on a grid
– the horizontal number is written before the vertical number
– they are written in brackets with a comma between

(3, 2) are the coordinates for the points on the grids.

cross-section

– what you see when an object is cut through

cube

– a 3D object which has six identical square faces

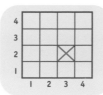

cubed number

– a number formed when another number is multiplied by itself three times

$$7 \times 7 \times 7 = 343 \quad (7^3 = 343)$$
343 is a cubed number.

cubic measure

– is used to measure volume
– measurements can be cubic centimetre (cm³); cubic metre (m³)

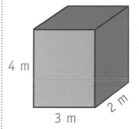

The volume of this box is 24 m³.

4 m

3 m

2 m

cylinder

– a 3D object that has two circular ends and a curved surface joining the ends

D

data
- a collection of information such as facts or measurements

What are the most popular fruits eaten by your friends?

This is the data.

Fruit	Number of people
orange	3
apple	4
plum	6
peach	10
grape	9
watermelon	12

date
- tells us what day, month and year it is

> 27th April 2007
> (short date 27/4/07)

day
- twenty-four hours which start and end at midnight

deca
- a prefix meaning ten

> decagon – a 10-sided figure
> decade – 10 years

decade
- 10 years

> 2000, 2001, 2002, 2003, 2004, 2005, 2006, 2007, 2008, 2009 make a decade.

decagon
- a polygon with ten straight sides

decimal
- based on the number 10

decimal fraction
- is a fraction written with a decimal point

> 0·65 and 4·8 are decimal fractions.

decrease
- to make smaller

The sand pile has decreased in size.

deduct
- to take away from

> Deduct $4 from your pay.
> (Take $4 away from your pay.)

degree

- a measurement used to measure angles
- also a measurement used to measure temperature
- uses the symbol °

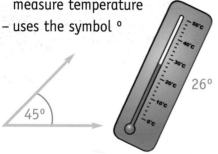

45°   26°

diagram

- a picture used to describe something

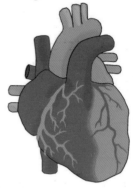

a diagram of a heart

denominator

- the bottom number in a common fraction

$\frac{1}{4}$ 4 is the denominator.

descending order

- in order from largest to smallest

204, 189, 132, 87, 31, 13
These numbers are written in descending order.

diameter

- a straight line drawn from one point on the circumference of a circle through the centre to another point on the circumference of the circle

diameter

diagonal

- a straight line that is drawn inside a shape from one vertex to another

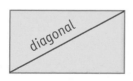

diagonal

diagonal

diamond

- another name for a rhombus

die (plural is dice)
– a numbered cube that is used in games

---

difference
– the amount by which one number is bigger or smaller than another number

> The difference between 7 and 11 is 4.

---

digit
– one of our numerals

> 0, 1, 2, 3, 4, 5, 6, 7, 8, 9
>
> are the digits we use.

---

digital clock (or watch)
– a clock or watch that has no hands
– they use numerals to show the time

digital clock

digital watch

dimension
– a measure of size

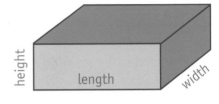

Length, height and width are dimensions.

---

direction
– the way something is placed or pointing

> Compass points, left, right, up, diagonally etc. are all directions.

The cat is to the left of the dog and north of the rabbit.

---

discount
– a reduction in money

> The discount is $2.

displacement
– how much water rises when an object is placed in it

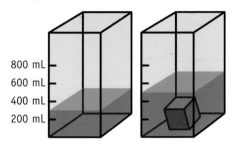

The displacement is 200 mL.

distance
– the length between two points

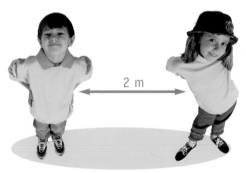

The distance between the children is 2 metres.

distributive law
3 × 8 + 3 × 4 is the same as
3 × (8 + 4) or 3 × 12.

2 × 7 + 9 × 7 = (2 + 9) × 7
= 11 × 7

divide
– to share something into groups

These 12 feathers are divided into 3 groups.

dividend
– the amount to be divided

36 ÷ 9 = 4

36 is the dividend.

division
– the act of dividing into groups

$$6 \overline{)\, 7\,2\,}^{\,1\,2}$$

divisor
– the number used to divide by

36 ÷ 9 = 4

9 is the divisor.

dodecagon
– a polygon with 12 straight sides

D

dominoes

- rectangular tiles with one face divided into two parts marked with dots
- used to play games

dot paper

- paper marked with a regular dot pattern
- can be square or isometric

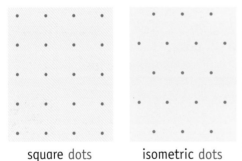

square dots   isometric dots

double

- make twice as many or twice as big

Double 6 is 12.
Double 3 kg is 6 kg.

dozen

- 12 things together

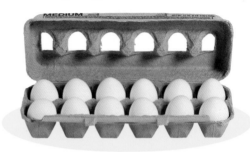

one dozen eggs

edge
– where two faces meet

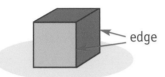

ellipse
– a curved shape like a squashed circle

enlarge
– to make something bigger

The orange has been enlarged.

equal
– exactly the same in value or size

$$6 + 3 \text{ is equal to } 9.$$
$$(6 + 3 = 9)$$
$$100 \text{ cm is equal to } 1 \text{ m.}$$
$$(100 \text{ cm} = 1 \text{ m})$$

equation
– a mathematical expression where one part is equal to another part
– an equal sign (=) is used

$$8 \times 2 = 12 + 4$$

equilateral triangle
– a triangle which has three equal sides
– its angles are all 60°

equivalent
– having the same value

is equivalent to

equivalent fractions
– fractions which have the same value

$\frac{1}{2}$ and $\frac{5}{10}$ are equivalent fractions.

estimate
– to make a close guess
– it is never an exact answer

> 215 + 683
>
> 900 is the estimation.

evaluate
– to work out the value

> $J - 5 = 9$ Evaluate for J.
>
> J = 14

even number
– a whole number that can be divided exactly by 2
– ends in 0, 2, 4, 6 or 8

> 112 is an even number.
>
> 221 is not an even number.

expanded notation
– writing a number to show the value of each digit

27 691 = 20 000 + 7 000 + 600 + 90 + 1

expression
– a string of numbers and symbols connected by operation signs

> $76 \div 4$ is an expression.
>
> $67 \times n - 42 \div 3$ is also an expression.

face
– a flat surface of a solid object

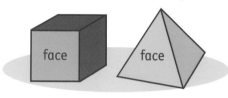

factor
– a whole number that divides exactly into another number

> $12 \div 4 = 3$ so 4 is a factor of 12.
> Other factors of 12 are
> 1, 2, 3, 6, 12.

Fibonacci sequence
– a sequence of numbers where each term, after the second term, is made by adding the previous two terms

> 1, 1, 2 (1 + 1), 3 (2 + 1),
> 5 (3 + 2), 8 (5 + 3) etc.
> 1, 1, 2, 3, 5, 8, 13, 21, 34, 55 ...

finite number
– a definite number
– can be counted

> There are a finite number of children in your school.
>
> There are a finite number of people in the world.

first
– comes before anything else

flip
– turn something over on one edge

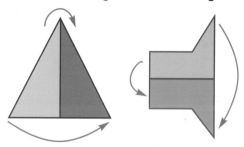

formula
– a rule
– shows how to work something out

> The formula for finding the area of a rectangle is $A = l \times b$.
>
> A stands for area, l for length and b for breadth.
>
>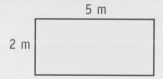
>
> $A = l \times b$
> $= 5 \times 2$
> $= 10 \text{ m}^2$

F

fortnight
– 2 whole weeks
– 14 days

fraction
– a part of a group or of a whole number

One car is circled. $\frac{1}{5}$

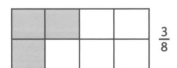
$\frac{3}{8}$

fraction bar
– the line that separates the numerator and the denominator

$\frac{2}{5}$ ⟵ fraction bar

frequency
– how often something happens

1	5	3	2
5	2	3	3
2	3	6	1
3	1	4	3

In this table:

3 has a frequency of 6.

4 has a frequency of 1.

geoboard

- a studded base board
- rubber bands are stretched around the studs to make shapes

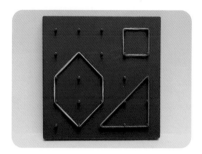

geometry

- a part of mathematics which deals with 2D and 3D space
- shapes, objects, size, position

googol

- is the number written as 1 followed by 100 zeros

$$10^{100}$$

gram

- a measurement used for weight
- 1 000 grams = 1 kilogram
- abbreviation is **g**

These strawberries weigh 250 g.

graph

- a diagram that shows a collection of data

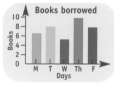

column graph   picture graph

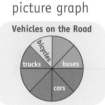

line graph   pie graph

greater than

- a symbol can be used to say greater than (>)

7 > 2 tells us that 7 is greater than 2.

gross

- twelve dozen or 144

gross mass

- the total mass; contents and container

grouping

- sharing objects into groups that are equal in size

15 beetles are shared into 3 groups.

handspan
- the distance between the tips of the thumb and little finger on an outstretched hand

hectare
- a measurement used to record large areas
- the abbreviation is **ha**

Fields are measured in hectares.

heft
- to feel the mass of an object by holding it in your hand

height
- the vertical distance from top to bottom

The height of the cubby house is I m 55 cm.

I m 55 cm

hemisphere
- half a sphere

heptagon
- a polygon that has 7 straight sides

hexagon
- a polygon that has six straight sides

Hindu-Arabic number system
- our number system
- was developed from the Hindus and Arabs
- uses numerals that include zero as a place keeper

0, 1, 2, 3, 4, 5, 6, 7, 8, 9

horizontal
- parallel to the horizon
- side to side

← horizon

This photo shows the horizon.

hour
- 60 minutes

The amount of time between 1 o'clock and 2 o'clock is one hour.

hundredth
- one part out of 100 parts

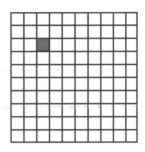

hypotenuse
- the side opposite the right angle in a right-angled triangle

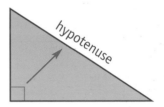

hypotenuse

Imperial system of measurement
– a system of weights and measures
– conforms to a set of standards made in England

> Imperial measures include feet, gallons, stones, ounces and acres.

improper fraction
– a fraction which has a numerator bigger than its denominator

> $\frac{3}{2}$ and $\frac{10}{7}$ are improper fractions.

increase
– to make something bigger

> The amount of water in the bowl will increase.

index (indices)
– a number that tells you how many times to multiply another number by itself
– a small number written to the right and above the base number

index number
3^2
3×3

5^3
$5 \times 5 \times 5$

infinite (adjective)
– never ending
– has no boundaries

> The set of even numbers is an infinite set. There is no last number.

infinity (noun)
– the state of being endless
– cannot be given an exact value
– uses the symbol ∞

integer
– is a whole number

> 7 is an integer.
> 315 is an integer.

intersect
– to cut across each other

This sign is used when roads intersect.

These are intersecting lines.

interval

– a part of a straight line
– has definite starting and ending
  points

A •————————————• B

The interval AB is 5 cm long.

irregular polygon

– sides are not equal in length
– angles are not equal in size

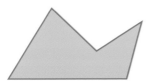

an irregular pentagon

isometric dot paper

isosceles triangle

– has two equal sides
– the angles opposite the equal
  sides are also equal

inverse

– in reverse

The inverse of multiplying by 7
is dividing by 7.

The inverse of adding 11 is
subtracting 11.

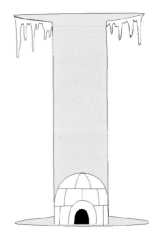

jump strategy

– an aid to mental addition or subtraction

– jump by parts of the number

$$147 + 58 = 147 + 50 + 3 + 5$$
$$= 197 + 3 + 5$$
$$= 200 + 5$$
$$= 205$$

key
- the information needed to read a picture graph or diagram

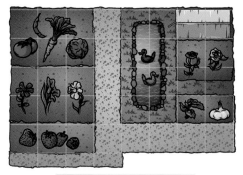

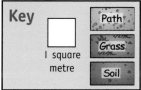

kilo
- a prefix meaning one thousand

> kilogram – 1 000 grams
> kilometre – 1 000 metres

kilogram
- a measure of mass
- abbreviation is **kg**

This dog weighs 7 kg.

kilolitre
- a measure for large amounts of fluid
- abbreviation is **kL**

An Olympic pool holds 1 000 kL of water.

kilometre
- a measure for long distances
- abbreviation is **km**

The length of a road is measured in kilometres.

kite
- a 4-sided 2D figure
- has two pairs of equal adjacent sides

leap year

– has 366 days

– in a leap year February has 29 days

– happens every 4th year

2024 is a leap year.
2028 is the next leap year.

February						
Sun	Mon	Tues	Wed	Thur	Fri	Sat
	1	2	3	4	5	6
7	8	9	10	11	12	13
14	15	16	17	18	19	20
21	22	23	24	25	26	27
28	29					

This calendar shows February
in a leap year.

least

– the smallest

The small bottle
holds the least oil.

length

– the distance from end to end

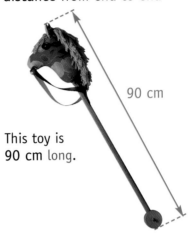

90 cm

This toy is
90 cm long.

less than

– a symbol can be used to say less
than (<)

13 < 29 tells us that
13 is less than 29.

line graph

– uses axes and lines to show data

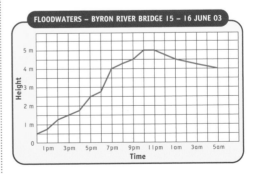

FLOODWATERS – BYRON RIVER BRIDGE 15 – 16 JUNE 03

lines

- parallel lines are straight lines that never meet no matter how far they are drawn
- perpendicular lines meet at right angles

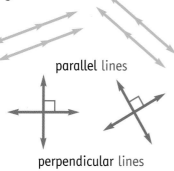

parallel lines

perpendicular lines

line symmetry

- a shape has line symmetry if both halves match exactly when it is folded on the line of symmetry
- line of symmetry is also called the axis of symmetry

line of
symmetry

litre

- a measure used for liquids
- abbreviation is L

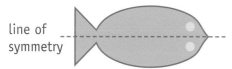

This bottle can measure 4 L.

lowest common denominator

- the lowest number that can be used for the denominator of a group of fractions

$$\frac{1}{2}, \frac{2}{3}, \frac{1}{6}, \frac{3}{4}$$

The lowest common denominator for this group is 12.

$$\frac{6}{12}, \frac{8}{12}, \frac{2}{12}, \frac{9}{12}$$

MAB blocks
– blocks used to show place value

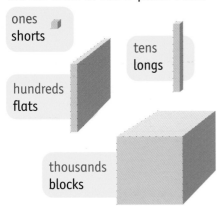

ones
shorts

tens
longs

hundreds
flats

thousands
blocks

---

magic square
– a square filled with numbers
– the numbers in each row, each column, each diagonal all have the same sum

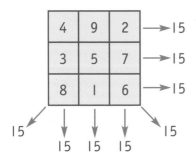

Each row, column and diagonal totals 15.

map
– a diagram of a country or place that shows its position in the world
– always drawn to scale

---

mass
– matter in an object
– is measured in grams, kilograms, tonnes

The mass of the fruit is 1 kg 385 g.

---

maximum
– the most

The maximum speed allowed is 60 kilometres per hour.

mean
– another name for average

9 kg   12 kg   19 kg   24 kg

The mean weight of these koalas
is 16 kg.

measure
– to work out the size or amount of
an object or distance

median
– the middle score (or scores) when
a set of scores are written in order
of size

Scores: 3, 3, 5, ⑦, 10, 10, 12
Median: 7

metre
– a measure used
for length or
distance
– abbreviation
is **m**

Running races
are measured
in metres.

metric system
– a system of measures based on
the decimal system
– in Australia we use the metric
system

Centimetre, metre, millilitre, litre,
tonne and gram are all measurements
used in the metric system.

millennium
– a thousand years

All the years from 2000 to 2999
make a millennium.

milli
– a prefix meaning one-thousandth

millimetre – one-thousandth of 1 metre
millilitre – one-thousandth of 1 litre

millilitre
– a measure used for small
amounts of liquid
– abbreviation is **mL**

30 mL
20 mL
10 mL
5 mL

Medicines are
measured in
millilitres.

millimetre
– a measure used for small lengths
– abbreviation is **mm**

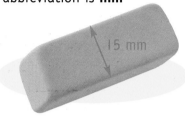
15 mm

This eraser is 15 millimetres wide.

million
– a thousand thousands

1 000 000

minimum
– the least amount

The minimum temperature for the last 24 hours was 0°C.

minus
– another word for subtract
– to take away

24 minus 7 is 17.

24 – 7 = 17

minute
– a measure of time
– 60 seconds is one minute

minute hand
– the large hand on a clock that tells the minutes
– it moves once around the clock face every hour

minute hand

mirror image
– an image which reflects another image exactly

mixed number
– has a whole number and a proper fraction

$6\frac{1}{2}$ is a mixed number.

whole number   proper fraction

mode
– is the score that occurs most often in a set of scores

> Scores: 4, 5, 7, 7, 8, 4, 7, 6, 5
> Mode: 7

model
– a small copy that shows what something looks like

a model train engine

month
– a measure of time
– 28, 29, 30 or 31 days
– there are 12 months in a year

> 30 days has September,
> April, June and November.
> All the rest have 31
> Except February alone,
> Which has 28 days clear
> And 29 days each leap year.

multiple
– the product of two or more factors

> 7 × 8 = 56
> 56 is a multiple of 7 and also of 8.

multiplicand
– the number being multiplied by another

> 6 × 9 = 54
> 6 is the multiplicand.

multiplication
– the total in a number of groups or rows

5 × 4 = 20

4 × 6 = 24

multiplier
– the number that is doing the multiplying

> 6 × 9 = 54
> 9 is the multiplier.

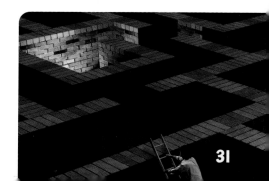

negative number
– a number less than zero

– written with a minus sign (–3 is negative three)

negative numbers   positive numbers

net
– a flat pattern that can be used to make a 3D object

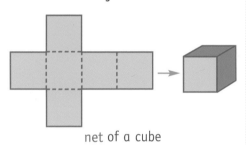

net of a cube

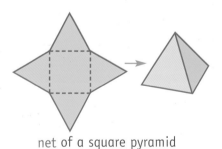

net of a square pyramid

net mass
– the mass of the contents not including the packaging

nonagon
– a polygon with 9 straight sides

notation
– a special way of writing numbers or mathematical expressions

Index notation uses indices to write numbers.

7^3 means $7 \times 7 \times 7$

nought
– a symbol that stands for zero

0

number line

– a line used to show the position of a number

– can start and end on any number

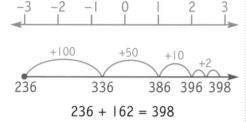

236 + 162 = 398

An open number line can help with addition.

number sentence

– a sentence written using numerals and signs

– shows a relationship between numbers

(7 – 4) × 8 = 24
is a number sentence.

numeral

– a symbol (or group of symbols) that stands for a number

0, 1, 2, 3, 4, 5, 6, 7, 8, 9
are the numerals we use in the metric system.

numerator

– the top number in a fraction

– tells us how many parts we have

$\frac{3}{8}$ 3 is the numerator.

It tells us that we have 3 eighths.

oblique
– slanting

This is an oblique line.

This is an oblique structure.

oblong
– another name for a rectangle that is not a square

obtuse angle
– is an angle larger than a right angle but smaller than a straight angle
– measures between 90° and 180°

octagon
– a polygon that has eight straight sides

odd number
– a number that cannot be divided exactly by two
– ends in 1, 3, 5, 7 or 9

> 15, 69, 441
> are all odd numbers.

odometer
– an instrument that measures distance travelled (as in a car)

operation
– one of the four methods of solving mathematical problems (+, –, ×, ÷)

> addition 5 + 7 + 9
> subtraction 259 – 165
> multiplication 28 × 36
> division 267 ÷ 13

ordering
– placing a group in order according to a given instruction, eg size, weight, length etc

These children are ordered according to height.

8, 23, 41, 88, 107
These numbers are in ascending order.

order of operations
– work everything inside brackets first
– then work all the × and ÷ from left to right
– lastly work all the + and – from left to right

$$7 \times (8 + 3) - 35 \div 7 = 7 \times 11 - 35 \div 7$$
$$= 77 - 5$$
$$= 72$$

ordinal number
– tells position
– 1st, 2nd, 3rd, 4th, 5th etc.

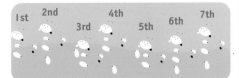

oval
– a closed curve that looks like a squashed circle

These sweets have an oval shape.

P

pair
- two together
- to make twos

a pair of shoes

palindrome
- reads the same backwards and forwards

676   1380831

palindromic numbers

parallel lines
- are two or more lines that will never meet no matter how far they are drawn

parallel lines

Train tracks are parallel.

parallelogram
- a special quadrilateral
- opposite sides are parallel
- opposite angles are equal

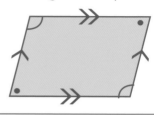

pattern
- numbers or objects that are arranged following a rule

1, 6, 11, 16, 21, 26
The rule is to add 5.

This pattern is made using triangles.

pattern blocks
- blocks that can be used to form patterns
- they are in many shapes

pentagon
– a polygon that has
  5 straight sides

percent (%)
– out of 100

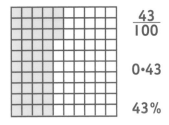

$\frac{43}{100}$

0·43

43%

perimeter
– the distance around the outside of
  a shape
– add the lengths of all the sides

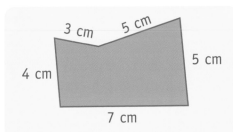

P = 4 cm + 3 cm + 5 cm + 5 cm + 7 cm

P = 24 cm

perpendicular
– at right angles to the horizon

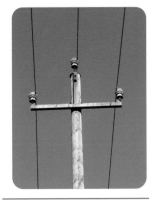

The pole and
cross bar are
perpendicular
to each other.

perpendicular lines
– lines that intersect at right angles

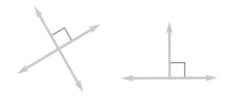

perpendicular lines

perspective
– the appearance of objects affected
  by size and position

This photograph of street lights
shows perspective.

P

pi (π)
- the ratio of the circumference of a circle to its diameter
- is equal to $\frac{22}{7}$
- does not have an exact decimal value (≈3·14)

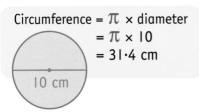

Circumference = π × diameter
= π × 10
= 31·4 cm

10 cm

picture graph
- uses pictures to represent data
- a key is used to interpret the pictures

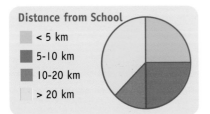

Taxis seen on the way home	
Adam	
Bill	
Martha	

Key = 2 taxis

pie graph
- drawn in a circle
- sectors are used to represent data

Distance from School
- < 5 km
- 5-10 km
- 10-20 km
- > 20 km

place value
- value according to place in a number

7 382

The place value of the 3 is *hundreds* because it is in the hundreds place.

The value of the 3 is 300.

plan
- a diagram that shows a view of the whole structure

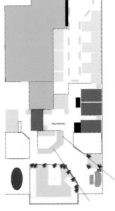

a floor plan of a house

plane shape
- a 2D shape that is drawn on a flat surface

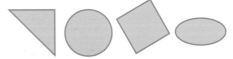

These are plane shapes.

platonic solids
- five regular polyhedra
- faces are regular polygons
- are named after Plato

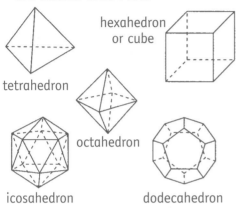

tetrahedron

hexahedron or cube

octahedron

icosahedron

dodecahedron

polygon
- a 2D shape with three or more sides and angles
- name comes from Greek words meaning many and angle

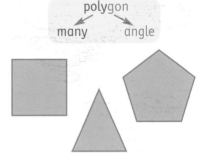

These are all polygons.

plus
- another word for add

50 cents plus 20 cents equals 70 cents.

pm
- stands for post meridiem
- means the time from midday to midnight (afternoon and evening)

polyhedron
- a solid object that has polygons as faces
- a regular polyhedron has all congruent faces
- pyramids and prisms are polyhedrons

P

polyomino

– a shape made from squares which are all the same size

Some polyominos are:

domino (2 squares)

triomino (3 squares)

tetromino (4 squares)

pentomino (5 squares)

position

– where something is placed in relation to things around it

The juice is in the glass.
The strawberries are on the plate.
The glass is behind the cup.

power of

– the power of a number is shown by an index number

– to find a power, a number is multiplied by itself a number of times

> 8^3 is 8 to the power of three.
> $(8 \times 8 \times 8)$
>
> 2^7 is 2 to the power of seven.
> $(2 \times 2 \times 2 \times 2 \times 2 \times 2 \times 2)$

prime factor

– a factor that is a prime number

> The prime factors of 12 are
> $2 \times 2 \times 3$.

prime number

– a number that has only two factors: itself and one

> 13 is a prime number.
> Its only factors are 1 and 13.

prism

– a 3D object

– it has two identical ends which give the prism its name

– all other faces are rectangles

a triangular prism

probability
- the chances of something happening
- words such as *possible*, *certain*, *unlikely*, *sure*, *impossible*, *most likely* etc. are used for probability

It is likely to rain tomorrow.
It is certain to rain this year.

problem
- a question that is answered by using mathematics
- some problems use words and some use only numbers

a number problem
98 × 12

Jo had 50 cherries and ate 34 of them. How many are left?

product
- the answer when two or more numbers are multiplied

7 × 3 = 21
21 is the product.

15 × 3 × 7 = 315
315 is the product.

proper fraction
- the numerator is smaller than the denominator

$\frac{1}{3}$, $\frac{2}{5}$, $\frac{8}{10}$, $\frac{21}{37}$
are all proper fractions.

protractor
- an instrument used to measure or draw angles

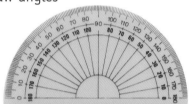

pyramid
- a 3D object
- it has one base which gives the pyramid its name
- all other faces are triangles

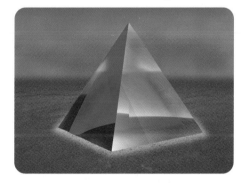

quadrant
- a quarter of a circle
- formed by two radii drawn at right angles to each other

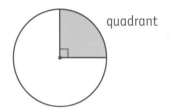

quadrant

quadrilateral
- a polygon with four straight sides

quarter
- one of four equal parts of a group or object
- written as $\frac{1}{4}$

$\frac{1}{4}$ of the square

$\frac{1}{4}$ of the wrenches

quotient
- the answer when one number is divided by another

$$36 \div 9 = 4$$

4 is the quotient

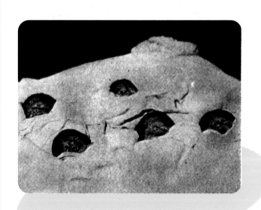

radius
– the distance from the centre of a circle to the circumference

random
– without any pattern or plan

choosing at random

range
– the difference between the lowest and highest scores in a group of scores

3, 6, 9, 1, 9, 4, 3, 5, 7
The range of this group of scores is (9 – 1) 8.

ratio (:)
– compares two or more like quantities

The ratio of cats to dogs is 1:3.

ray
– part of a straight line
– it has a definite starting point but no end

ray

rectangle
– a special quadrilateral
– all angles are right angles
– opposite sides are equal

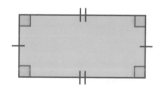

R

recurring decimal
– some numbers in the decimal keep repeating
– the repeating numbers have repeating dots over them
– a never-ending decimal

$$\frac{1}{3} \ (1 \div 3) = 0 \cdot 33333333333333 \text{ etc.}$$
$$= 0 \cdot \dot{3}$$
$$\frac{3}{11} \ (3 \div 11) = 0 \cdot 2727272727 \text{ etc.}$$
$$= 0 \cdot \dot{2}\dot{7}$$

reduce
– to make smaller

Slow down! The speed must become smaller.

reflection
– a shape or object as seen in a mirror

reflex angle
– an angle that measures between 180° and 360°

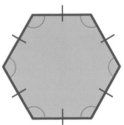

regular polygon
– a polygon that has all sides equal
– it also has all angles equal

This is a regular hexagon.

remainder
– the amount left over when one number cannot be divided exactly by another

17 ÷ 7 = 2 with 3 left over
3 is the remainder.

revolution
– an angle that measures 360°
– a complete turn through 4 right angles
– the arms are together

rhombus

– a special quadrilateral
– all sides are equal
– opposite sides are parallel
– opposite angles are equal

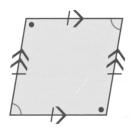

right angle

– an angle that measures 90°

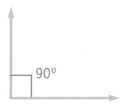

90°

right-angled triangle

– a triangle that has one right
  angle

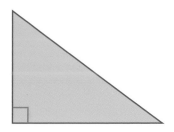

Roman numerals

– a number system used by the
  ancient Romans
– I, V, X, L, C, D, M are the symbols
  used

MDCLXX = 1 670

This clock has
Roman numerals.

rotational symmetry

– when a shape looks the same in
  different positions as it is turned
  at a fixed point, it has rotational
  symmetry

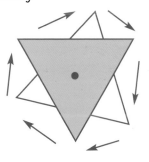

45

rounding off

- giving an approximate answer
- numerals 0, 1, 2, 3, 4 let the number being rounded to, remain unchanged
- numerals 5, 6, 7, 8, 9 tell you to + 1 to the number being rounded to

> Round to the nearest hundred.
>
> $4\ 539 \approx 4\ 500$
>
> (because 3 lets the hundreds numeral remain unchanged)
>
> $7\ 264 \approx 7\ 300$
>
> (because the numeral 6 tells us to +1 to the hundreds numeral)

---

row

- numbers or objects in a horizontal line

> 2, 4, 6, 8, 10, 12
>
> A row of even numbers.

> A row of paper people.

rule

- an instruction that applies to a sequence of numbers or a pattern

> 1, 2, 4, 8, 16
>
> Rule: double to get the new term.

> Rule: turn shape 90° clockwise.

scale

– the ratio of the length shown to the real length it represents

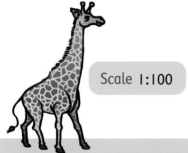

Scale 1:100

The picture is 4 cm high so the giraffe is really 400 cm high.

scale drawing

– enlarging or decreasing the size of a drawing to a given scale

scalene triangle

– a triangle that has sides of different lengths
– the angles are different sizes

4 cm   2 cm

5 cm

scales

– instruments used to weigh objects
– also used to compare masses

season

– there are 4 seasons in a year: Spring, Summer, Autumn, Winter
– each season is 3 months long

Spring: September, October, November
(91 days)

Summer: December, January, February
(90 or 91 days)

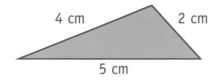

47

S

Autumn: March, April, May (92 days)

Winter: June, July, August (92 days)

second
– a very short measure of time
– there are 60 seconds in 1 minute

section
– a part of a whole

These are sections of mandarin.

sector
– a part of a circle bounded by two radii and an arc

segment
– a part of a circle bounded by a chord and an arc

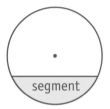

semicircle
– half a circle

septagon
– another name for a 2D shape with seven straight sides

sequence
– a list of numbers or objects which are in a special order

> 1, 1, 2, 3, 5, 8, 13 ...
> This is a special sequence called the Fibonacci sequence.

set
– a collection of objects or numbers
– each member is called an element of the set

> Spring, Summer, Autumn, Winter
> This is the set of seasons in a year.

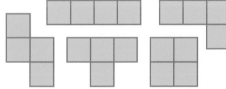

This is the set of tetrominos.

set square
– an instrument shaped like a right-angled triangle
– it can be used to draw right angles
– it can also be used to draw parallel lines

sharing
– putting into equal groups or parts

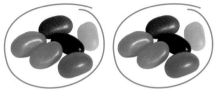

These 12 sweets are shared into two equal groups.

side
– one of the lines that form a 2D shape

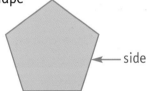

side

A pentagon has 5 sides.

side view
– what you see when you look at an object from the side

sign
– a symbol used instead of words

> +, %, >, π, √, ≈
> These are some signs we use in maths.

size
– how big an object is

A lion is a large cat.

skip counting
– to count on or to count back in groups of the same size

10, 15, 20, 25, 30
This is skip counting on in groups of 5.

20, 17, 14, 11, 8
This is skip counting back in groups of 3.

slide
– to move a shape without lifting it
– it has no change in direction or placement of features

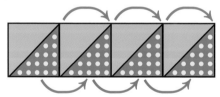

solid
– an object that has three dimensions: length, height and width

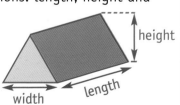

sort
– to place things into like groups

These are sorted into fruits and vegetables.

fruits

vegetables

speed
– how fast something is moving

This rollercoaster is travelling at 75 kilometres per hour (75 km/h).

sphere
– a 3D object shaped like a ball

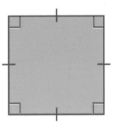

spinner
– a disc that can be spun to show numbers or colours at random
– it is used in games of chance

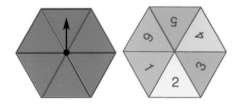

spiral
– an open curve that winds around
– can be endless

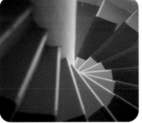

spring
– the season that follows winter
– September, October, November

square
– a polygon with four equal sides and four right angles

square measure
– is the measurement used when finding area

The area of a tennis court is measured in square metres.

square number
– when a number is multiplied by itself the answer is a square number
– a square number can always form a square pattern

7 × 7 = 49
49 is a square number.

7 × 7 =

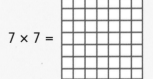

square root (√)

– of a given number is the number that when multiplied by itself, makes the given number

$$\sqrt{81} = 9 \text{ because } 9 \times 9 = 81$$

straight angle

– an angle which looks like a straight line

– always measures 180° (2 right angles)

straight line

– the shortest distance between two points

The shortest distance between Smelly Swamp and Golden Sands is the line AB.

strategy

– a method for working something out

$$73 \times 4$$

A good strategy for multiplying by 4 is to double and double again.

73 doubled = 146 and
146 doubled = 292
so 73 × 4 = 292

statistics

– facts and figures presented in numbers

– information is collected by survey

subitising

– being able to say how many are in a group without counting

Without counting you know there are 5 children in this group.

subtract

– to take one number away from another

$$12 - 7 = 5$$

sum
– the total when numbers are added

$$3 + 5 + 9 = 17$$
17 is the sum of 3, 5 and 9.

summer
– the season that follows spring
– December, January, February

supplementary angles
– two angles that total 180°
– together they make a straight angle

120° / 60°

60° and 120° are
supplementary angles.

77° \ 103°

103° and 77° are
supplementary angles.

surface
– the top or outside layer of an object
– it can be flat or curved

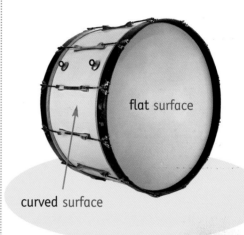

flat surface

curved surface

surface area
– the total area of all the surfaces of a 3D object

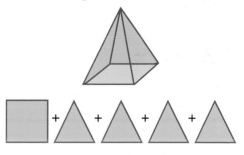

The surface area of this square pyramid is the area of the square base plus the areas of the four triangular sides.

survey
– to collect facts or data about a topic

Sport	Tally	Total
Tennis	⟋⟋⟋⟋ ⟋⟋⟋⟋ ⟋⟋⟋⟋ ⟋⟋⟋⟋ ‖	22
Cricket	⟋⟋⟋⟋ ⟋⟋⟋⟋ ⟋⟋⟋⟋	15
Basketball	⟋⟋⟋⟋ ⟋⟋⟋⟋ ⟋⟋⟋⟋ ‖‖	18
Rugby	⟋⟋⟋⟋ ⟋⟋⟋⟋ ⟋⟋⟋⟋ ⟋⟋⟋⟋ ‖‖‖	24
Golf	⟋⟋⟋⟋ ⟋⟋⟋⟋ ⟋⟋⟋⟋ ⟋⟋⟋⟋ ‖	21

100 people were surveyed about their favourite sport.

symbol
– a sign or letter used instead of words

> $+$ (plus), π (pi), $\sqrt{}$ (square root), $\neq$ (is not equal to)

symmetry
– when one half of a shape is a reflection of the other half
– when folded on an axis of symmetry the two halves fit exactly on top of each other

axis of symmetry

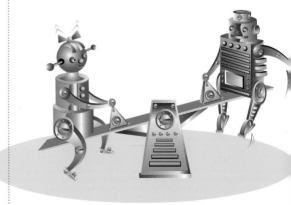

table
– numbers or quantities arranged in rows and columns

SNACK AROUND THE WORLD

	Hotdog	Coffee	Hamburger
New York	$2.50	$1.75	$3.10
Hong Kong	$4.25	$3.95	$6.40
Vancouver	$3.35	$2.85	$4.50
London	£3.00	£4.00	£5.10
Singapore	$3.35	$1.95	$3.90

tables
– a short name for all the multiplication facts

take away
– to find the difference between two things or numbers

17 take away 9
$17 - 9 = 8$

tally
– to count how many there are

tally marks
– marks used to help when counting a large number
– they are drawn in bundles of five

|||| |||| |||| |||| |||| ||| = 28

tangram
– a traditional Chinese puzzle
– a square cut into one parallelogram, one square and five triangles

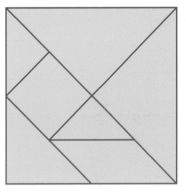

temperature
– how hot or cold a thing is

The temperature is hot.

The temperature is cold.

term
– one of the parts (elements) of a sequence

> 4, 8, 12, 16, 20
> 8 is the second term in this sequence.

tessellation
– a pattern made of identical shapes
– the shapes fit together without any gaps
– the shapes do not overlap

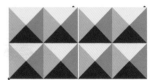

This tessellating pattern is made with triangles.

This tessellating pattern is made with squares.

tetrahedron
– a polyhedron that has four faces

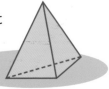

thermometer
– an instrument used to measure temperature

three-dimensional
– an object that has height, width and depth

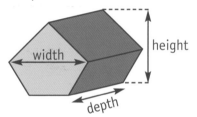
width
height
depth

time
– the space between one event and the next
– the space taken by an action

It takes Tom 17 minutes to eat breakfast.

time line
- a diagram used to show the length of time between things happening

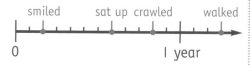

timetable
- a table where times are organised for when things happen
- examples are bus timetables, school timetables, TV timetables

Train Timetable			
Departure			Station
A	B	C	
20:43	06:58	12:53	Sydney
20:54	07:09	13:04	Strathfield
21:26	07:41	13:36	Campbelltown
22:31	08:46	14:41	Moss Vale
23:19	09:34	15:29	Goulburn

times
- another word for multiply

3 times 8 is the same as 3 × 8

tonne
- a unit of mass
- 1 000 kilograms = 1 tonne
- abbreviation is **t**

An elephant can weigh 7 tonnes.

top view
- what you see when you view an object from directly above it

the top view of a cup of coffee

total
- add all the numbers to find the total

5 + 19 + 32 + 6 + 18 = 80

80 is the total.

57

trading
– changing a number into smaller or bigger parts

10 shorts make 1 long.
10 ones make 1 ten.

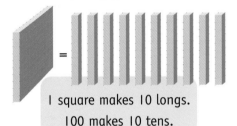

1 square makes 10 longs.
100 makes 10 tens.

transformation
– moving a shape so that the shape does not change but it is in a different position
– flip, slide or turn can be used for a transformation

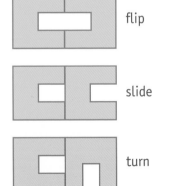

flip

slide

turn

trapezium
– a special quadrilateral
– one pair of opposite sides are parallel

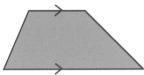

treble
– to make something three times bigger
– multiply by three

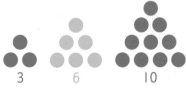

The number of strawberries has trebled.

triangle
– a polygon with three straight sides

triangular number
– a number that can make a triangular dot pattern

3   6   10

3, 6, 10 are triangular numbers.

trundle wheel
– an instrument used to measure lengths

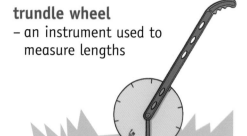

turn
– to rotate about a point

P is turning.

turning symmetry
– see rotational symmetry

twelve-hour time
– time is told in 12-hour lots
– 12 midnight to 12 noon is from midnight to midday (morning) and is am time.
– 12 noon to 12 midnight is from midday to midnight (afternoon and night) and is pm time.

9 o'clock in the morning is 9 am.
9 o'clock in the evening is 9 pm.

twenty-four hour time
– time is told in 24-hour lots (1 day = 24 hours)
– 4 digits are used

9:30 am in 24-hour time is written as 0930 or 09:30.
2:45 pm in 24-hour time is written as 1445 or 14:45.

two-dimensional
– a shape that only has two dimensions; length and width (height)

width

length

height

length

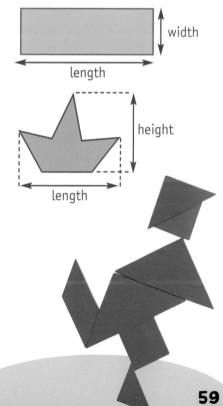

U

unequal (≠)
– not equal to

$$7 + 4 \neq 5 + 8$$

unit
– a unit is one
– units are recorded in the ONES column

Hundreds	Tens	Ones
	3	7

3 tens and 7 units

units of measurement
– standard units used for comparison

Units of length are millimetre, centimetre, metre, kilometre.

Units of time are second, minute, hour, day, week, month, year, decade.

value
– what something is worth

The value of the coin is twenty cents.

◆ + 4 = 10
The value of ◆ is 6.

variable
– a quantity which is represented by a symbol and can have different values

■ + ★ = 6

■ and ★ are variables.
They can have many values,
eg ■ = 1 and ★ = 5 or
■ = 4 and ★ = 2.

vertex
– the point where two or more straight lines meet

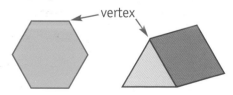
vertex

vertical
– at right angles to the horizon

The tree trunks are vertical.

vinculum
– the line in a fraction, that separates the numerator and denominator

$$\frac{2}{5} \longleftarrow \text{vinculum}$$

volume
– the amount of space an object occupies

Volume = 2 × 2 × 2
= 8 cubic units

Units of volume:
cubic centimetres (cm³)
cubic metres (m³)

week

- a time period of seven days
- Sunday, Monday, Tuesday, Wednesday, Thursday, Friday, Saturday

weight

- the heaviness of an object

Sweets are often sold by weight.

whole

- all of something
- a whole number does not include a fraction or decimal

6, 94, 1 053
are all whole numbers.

width

- how wide a thing is

The width of this CD is 12 cm.

12 cm

winter

- the season that follows autumn
- June, July, August

X

x

- the letter x is often used in algebra to stand for an unknown number

$$4 + x = 9$$
$$so\ x = 5$$

Y

year

- a time period of 12 months
- starts on 1st January and ends on 31st December
- has 365 days in a normal year and 366 days in a leap year
- Earth makes one complete revolution around the sun in one year.

Each new year starts on 1st January.

Z

zero

- a place keeper
- has no value

0

Symbols

$+$	add	π	pi ($\approx 3\cdot14$)
$-$	subtract	$^\circ$	degree
$\times$	multiply	$^\circ$C	degree Celsius
$\div$	divide	∞	infinity

$<$	less than	$\leftrightarrow$	line
$>$	more than	$\perp$	perpendicular to
$\leq$	less than or equal to	⌐	right angle
$\geq$	more than or equal to		parallel lines
$=$	equal to		lines of equal length
$\neq$	not equal to		
$\approx$	approximately equal to		
$\therefore$	therefore		

brackets

$(\ )$	parenthesis
$[\ ]$	square brackets
$\{\ \}$	braces

^{2}	(7^2) squared
^{3}	(7^3) cubed
$\sqrt{}$	square root
$\sqrt[3]{}$	cube root

$\%$	percent
$\cdot$	($6\cdot4$) decimal point

Abbreviations

mm	millimetre	am	anti meridiem (morning)
cm	centimetre	pm	post meridiem (afternoon, evening)
m	metre		
km	kilometre		
mm²	square millimetre		
cm²	square centimetre		
m²	square metre		
km²	square kilometre		
ha	hectare		
cm³	cubic centimetre		
m³	cubic metre		

g	gram
kg	kilogram
t	tonne

mL	millilitre
L	litre
kL	kilolitre

Equivalent fraction/decimal/percentage table

Fraction	Decimal	Percentage
$\frac{1}{2}$	0·5	50%
$\frac{1}{3}$	0·$\dot{3}$	$33\frac{1}{3}$%
$\frac{1}{4}$	0·25	25%
$\frac{3}{4}$	0·75	75%
$\frac{1}{5}$	0·2	20%
$\frac{2}{5}$	0·4	40%
$\frac{3}{5}$	0·6	60%
$\frac{4}{5}$	0·8	80%
$\frac{1}{8}$	0·125	$12\frac{1}{2}$%
$\frac{3}{8}$	0·375	$37\frac{1}{2}$%
$\frac{1}{10}$	0·1	10%
$\frac{1}{20}$	0·05	5%
$\frac{1}{100}$	0·01	1%

Roman numerals

I	= 1	**VI**	= 6
II	= 2	**VII**	= 7
III	= 3	**VIII**	= 8
IV	= 4	**IX**	= 9
V	= 5	**X**	= 10

X	= 10	**LX**	= 60
XX	= 20	**LXX**	= 70
XXX	= 30	**LXXX**	= 80
XL	= 40	**XC**	= 90
L	= 50	**C**	= 100

C	= 100	**DC**	= 600
CC	= 200	**DCC**	= 700
CCC	= 300	**DCCC**	= 800
CD	= 400	**CM**	= 900
D	= 500	**M**	= 1 000

Measurement

Length
10 mm = 1 cm
100 cm = 1 m
1 000 m = 1 km

Mass
1 000 g = 1 kg
1 000 kg = 1 t

Capacity
1 000 mL = 1 L
1 000 L = 1 kL

Area
100 mm^2 = 1 cm^2
10 000 cm^2 = 1 m^2
10 000 m^2 = 1 ha
100 ha = 1 km^2

Time
60 seconds = 1 minute
60 minutes = 1 hour
24 hours = 1 day
7 days = 1 week
14 days = 2 weeks = 1 fortnight
365 days = 1 year
366 days = 1 leap year
12 months = 1 year
10 years = 1 decade
100 years = 1 century
1 000 years = 1 millennium

Days in months
30 days has September,
April, June and November.
All the rest have 31
Except February alone,
Which has 28 days clear
And 29 days each leap year.

Conversion tables

Converting from Imperial measurement to Metric measurement and vice versa (correct to two decimal places)

Length

Imperial to Metric

1 inch (in)	2·54 centimetre (cm)
1 foot (ft)	30·48 cm
1 yard (yd)	0·91 metre (m)
1 mile	1·61 kilometre (km)

Metric to Imperial

1 cm	0·39 in
1 m	1·09 yd
1 km	0·62 mile

Area

Imperial to Metric

1 acre	4 046·87 m²
	0·40 hectare (ha)

Metric to Imperial

1 ha	2·47 acres

Capacity

Imperial to Metric

1 fluid ounce	28·41 millilitre (mL)
1 pint (pt)	0·57 litre (L)
1 gallon (gal)	4·55 L

Metric to Imperial

1 L	1·76 pt

Mass

Imperial to Metric

1 ounce (oz)	28·35 gram (g)
1 pound (lb)	0·45 kilogram (kg)
1 stone	6·35 kg
1 ton	1·02 tonne (t)

Metric to Imperial

1 g	0·04 oz
1 kg	2·20 lb
1 t	0·98 ton

Polygons

Regular polygons

triangle has 3 sides

quadrilateral has 4 sides

pentagon has 5 sides

hexagon has 6 sides

heptagon has 7 sides

octagon has 8 sides

nonagon has 9 sides

decagon has 10 sides

Special quadrilaterals

square
- all sides equal
- all angles equal

rectangle
- opposite sides
  equal
- all angles right angles

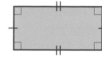

rhombus
- all sides equal
- opposite sides
  parallel
- opposite angles equal

parallelogram
- opposite sides
  equal and parallel
- opposite angles
  equal

trapezium
- one pair of opposite
  sides parallel

kite
- two pairs of equal,
  adjacent sides

Parts of a circle

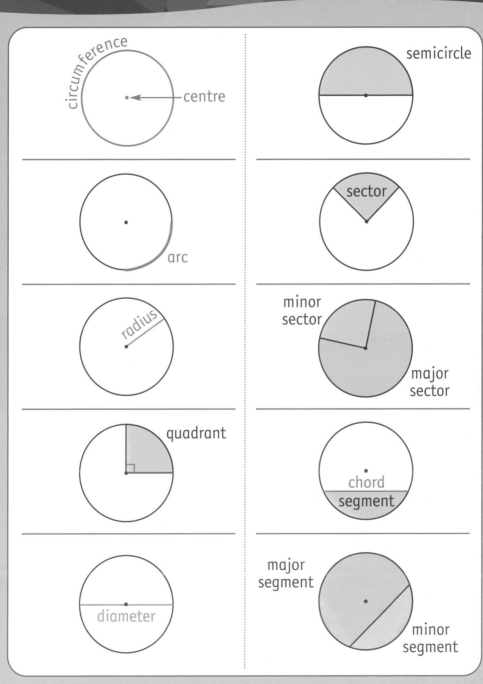

circumference

centre

semicircle

arc

sector

radius

minor sector

major sector

quadrant

chord

segment

diameter

major segment

minor segment

Angles

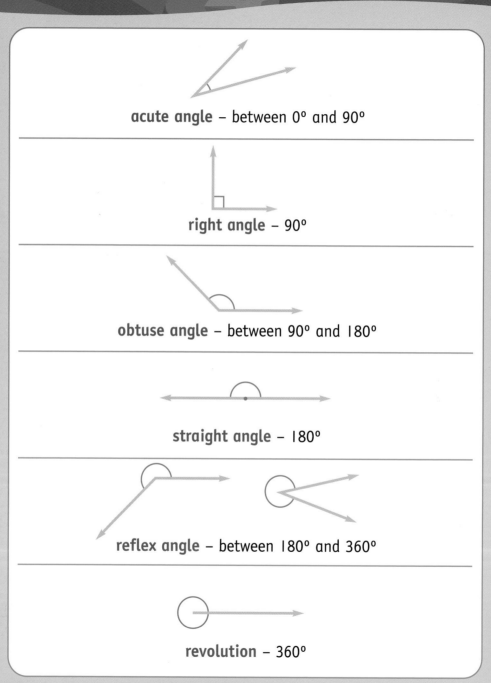

acute angle – between 0° and 90°

right angle – 90°

obtuse angle – between 90° and 180°

straight angle – 180°

reflex angle – between 180° and 360°

revolution – 360°

Triangles

Scalene triangle
- all sides are different lengths
- all angles are different sizes

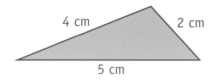

Isosceles triangle
- two sides are equal lengths
- the angles opposite the equal sides are equal in size

Equilateral triangle
- all sides are equal lengths
- all angles are equal in size (60°)

Right-angled triangle
- one angle is a right angle

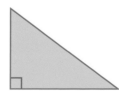

Angle sum
- the three angles always total 180°

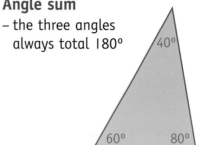

Hypotenuse
- is the side opposite the right angle

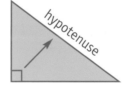

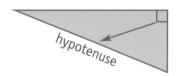

3D objects

sphere

cone

cylinder

hemisphere

cube

rectangular prism

triangular prism

hexagonal prism

triangular pyramid

square pyramid

pentagonal pyramid

rectangular pyramid

Squared and cubed numbers

Squares

$1^2 = 1$

$2^2 = 4$

$3^2 = 9$

$4^2 = 16$

$5^2 = 25$

$6^2 = 36$

$7^2 = 49$

$8^2 = 64$

$9^2 = 81$

$10^2 = 100$

Square roots

$\sqrt{1} = 1$

$\sqrt{4} = 2$

$\sqrt{9} = 3$

$\sqrt{16} = 4$

$\sqrt{25} = 5$

$\sqrt{36} = 6$

$\sqrt{49} = 7$

$\sqrt{64} = 8$

$\sqrt{81} = 9$

$\sqrt{100} = 10$

Cubes

$1^3 = 1$

$2^3 = 8$

$3^3 = 27$

$4^3 = 64$

$5^3 = 125$

$6^3 = 216$

$7^3 = 343$

$8^3 = 512$

$9^3 = 729$

$10^3 = 1\ 000$

Cube roots

$\sqrt[3]{1} = 1$

$\sqrt[3]{8} = 2$

$\sqrt[3]{27} = 3$

$\sqrt[3]{64} = 4$

$\sqrt[3]{125} = 5$

$\sqrt[3]{216} = 6$

$\sqrt[3]{343} = 7$

$\sqrt[3]{512} = 8$

$\sqrt[3]{729} = 9$

$\sqrt[3]{1\ 000} = 10$

Prime numbers to 100

1	2	3	4	5	6	7	8	9	10
11	12	13	14	15	16	17	18	19	20
21	22	23	24	25	26	27	28	29	30
31	32	33	34	35	36	37	38	39	40
41	42	43	44	45	46	47	48	49	50
51	52	53	54	55	56	57	58	59	60
61	62	63	64	65	66	67	68	69	70
71	72	73	74	75	76	77	78	79	80
81	82	83	84	85	86	87	88	89	90
91	92	93	94	95	96	97	98	99	100